DAYS OF SPIRIT

AIR

SANFRANCISCOBOOKS.US

Days of Spirit. Air

ISBN-13: 978-1536894806
ISBN-10: 153689480X

Cover: ONE OF WIND. DAWN, from *Tarot of the Spirit,*
painted by Joyce Eakins, © U.S. Games, Inc. Used by permission.

THE
AIR
JOURNAL

The dark clouds of your mind are scattered, blown away by a strong Wind at daybreak. A new idea takes hold. A Light turns on in your life. Pay attention to New Thought. This is a time of activation.

Tarot of the Spirit, 1 of Wind

AIR

Wind represents the inflow of breath, the very force of life. It is the Wind moving in and out of the body. It is the moment of birth, when the word becomes flesh, the cutting edge and the point where all ideas and potential are released into the world. This is the moment of sudden recognition; the time of rejoicing, when the child calls out "I AM!"

Tarot of the Spirit, 1 of Wind

AIR

T he human world, quite simply, is a symbolic universe that is driven by the Power of Symbolization. Our very consciousness is shaped, in large part, by this Power. For example, we are born with the potential to become part of or embrace any language, any religion, or any culture. A two-year-old makes universal sounds that become shaped into a specific language by his or her surroundings. Shaping sounds: that is our power.

What sounds will *you* shape?

Visionary Cosmology

AIR

The Cosmos is a charged field. We move into the cosmological field – as electrified Cosmos – and align ourselves with cosmological energies. Cosmological alignment creates sudden illumination as all that has been concealed is suddenly revealed in the Lightning Flash of insight. This is, in effect, like plugging in a power cord. The unknown appears; becomes clarified and bright. Here is a high energy period for initiating change, a time of rapid movement and intense growth.

Kabbalah and Tarot of the Spirit, 8 of Fire

AIR

The simplicity of the fast food logo makes it an *efficacious symbol*. When a symbol is simple, it is easier to remember. Efficacious symbolism is an aspect of *causal efficacy*. To be causally efficacious is to be effective at bringing about change.

Visionary Cosmology

AIR

W hen you come to this point, you know, without a doubt, that you are manifest Cosmos creating Self, environment and future. Now you know, without a doubt, that you, yourself, are a cosmological creative power. Now you know that it is your charge to act responsibly. The immensity of your creative power is thrilling, yet it can also be daunting. Change disrupts. Heightened awareness is required. Honor Self as Cosmos. Enact the adventure with balance, compassion and cosmological alignment.

Kabbalah and Tarot of the Spirit, 2 of Earth

AIR

I perceive my body as force and form in rapid movement. I ask the question, "Who Am I?" The Council is present. With their help, the answer is revealed: I AM Eternal Cosmos.

Kabbalah and Tarot of the Spirit, 2 of Earth

AIR

Y ou are learning the great secret. The great secret is the
balanced and harmonious establishment of material
energy. Harmonious means that influence – fully perceived – is
coming from the higher consciousness.

Tarot of the Spirit, 6 of Earth

AIR

Listen to your conscience. Trust in your impulses. Be guided by your instincts and intuition. You are in a gentle and sensitive period. It is like falling in love all over again.

Tarot of the Spirit, Water Father

AIR

P erseverance, commitment and discipline are the real keys to success. Talent is important, but not the most important factor. You are learning, practicing, growing and blossoming. This is a good time to be an eager student. It is as if you are climbing a great mountain in your life. The way may seem steep and rocky, but you will get there if you walk one step at a time. The important thing is not the view from the top, but how you feel during each step on the path.

Tarot of the Spirit, 8 of Earth

AIR

H e is the Sun Warrior, the comet of Spirit and
Consciousness, forming as brilliant light streaking
across the cosmological stage. He seeks his cause even as he
becomes it. He releases that which holds him back – he
releases dysfunctional relationships – in favor of greater
awareness, which is why he is such a splendid activist when it
comes to social, environmental and cosmological justice.

Kabbalah and Tarot of the Spirit, Fire Brother

AIR

W e can and do change our perception of possibility by casting new symbols into our technologies, texts, traditions, beliefs and ideologies. We can and do change our perception of possibility by changing the form of our interpersonal, organizational and institutional interactions.

Visionary Cosmology

AIR

W e can change our symbolic languages. We can create new concepts such as David Bohm's *implicate order* and *holomovement*, Mohandas Gandhi's *satyagraha*, Carl Jung's *collective unconscious*, John L. Sullivan's *manifest destiny*, Martin Luther King's *beloved community* and Anastasia West's/Pamela Eakins' *panoriginal field* and *erotomorphic world*. We can invent a symbol for nuclear disarmament, a sign for peace that can be understood the world over:

Visionary Cosmology

AIR

N ed continued, "Socrates said the truest answer for all questions is to know thyself." Indigo Lorenzo listened attentively. If the task was to know thyself, and to become a knower of the field, the internal field, maybe she had been born under a good sign after all. She knew she was very capable of studying her own deep internal being.

The Lightning Papers, Ned Lee; Indigo Lorenzo

AIR

"I think if we meditated on our own thoughts and our own behavior, especially emotions like anger, we could be instructed and see how we could go deeper to find out where the real problems lie. If we did that search with love as our highest value, we would see the whole picture completely differently." Natalie could feel the river washing her clean, even now.

The Lightning Papers, Natalie Pono

AIR

E arth Father appears to me as White Eagle Man, my personal guide. White Eagle Man has taught me so much because he has come from the intense materialistic interior of my culture and expanded into the all-compassionate and all-embracing Infinite. Humbly, with few words, he demonstrates the way. I call upon him. I feel his presence. I ask, Is there anything I need to know now? I hear the word Emergence. I realize I am a place of Emergence in the steaming spring.

Kabbalah and Tarot of the Spirit, Earth Father

AIR

A spiritual connection ignites as power finds a home. Charged Impulse, Directed Energy, Focused Action, Encounter, Connection, Seized Opportunity, Risk-taking, Convergence, Alliance. Stay the Path. Your Heart has Found a Home. You are in the right place at the right time. Keep on and your courage in starting an enterprise will eventually pay off. Just remember, in order to prosper, you must stay attuned to Cosmic Love.

Kabbalah and Tarot of the Spirit, 2 of Fire

AIR

T he Cosmological Power of Attraction draws together and coheres the enveloping universe as well as the universe(s) within all that exists. When two attracted points move into proximity with one another, their spheres overlap. In medieval times, the overlapping area was referred to as the *vesica piscis*. The vesica piscis, they said, was the womb or eye-shaped portal through which the universe emerged into manifestation.

Visionary Cosmology

AIR

C apturing or describing a moment through symbols –
languages, images, numbers – enables us not only to
remember but to create further codes, symbols and systems by
which to set a desired course of action in motion. At every
level we continue to learn and learn again.

What code will you create?

Visionary Cosmology

AIR

D o not deny the consequences of your actions. Own the results of your thoughts, words and deeds. For even thought constitutes action in the energy cycles of the universe. Adjust your actions and embrace love. Remember these words: "Whatsoever a man soweth, that shall he also reap."

Tarot of the Spirit, Karma

AIR

Y ou are in a temporary balance which may feel like a state of *detente*. There is a sense of release from captivity. Maintain balance gently and peace can continue. Use all of your wisdom and understanding to assess the situation.

Tarot of the Spirit, 2 of Wind

AIR

T he Ocean hits upon the Shore rising to ebb to rise once more. The Crane stands on one stilt, retreating in Dark Waters. The Star is a White Dwarf and a Red Giant. There is no contradiction. This is the balance that regulates the Energy bursting from the Power of Recognition.

Tarot of the Spirit, 2 of Wind

AIR

L isten to the stillness at the Center of the Cyclone, the calm crevice of Truth. Truth breathes hollowly, sends chills, dispels illusion by the still, cool air of the Moon. There is Truth at the breathy core. Whirling, twirling, the Dance of Karma swirls off excess costume like tattered fringe-lace on the dancer's dress, casting of excess bit by bit, until remains a breathless core which lives and learns and breathes and grows from one life to the next – without expectation.

Tarot of the Spirit, Karma

AIR

The Dance of Karma spins and whirls like the twirling of a little girl learning balance; whirling with glittering Magic Sword and Wand, finding skill and lore, spinning madly about that which is still – the empty breathy Center – sighing *Love is the Law, Love under Will,* breathing *Love is the Will, Love under Law.*

Tarot of the Spirit, Karma

AIR

R ead the writing on the wall, people. The fire and ice of his fundamentalism says it all. Things are getting so rigid, they're bound to crack open soon.

The Lightning Papers, Jack Jackson

AIR

Since he'd gone to college and become aware, this sense of entitlement that he learned about, this *Manifest Destiny,* had been hard on Jim's stomach. *They even make codes against building with straw and adobe, biodegradable, natural, durable, cheap – what's that about? They even have a law against collecting rain from your own roof.* Sadly, he remembered how his dad had to blow up the sacred lands for the Winchester Shale Mine – just to make a living.

The Lightning Papers, Jim Wing

AIR

W andering in and out of remembering he was walking the Edge of the World, Jim Wing reviewed the stages of the Cenozoic Era. *Starts 65 million years ago – after the death of the dinosaurs. Hominids., homo sapiens, us.* Suddenly, Jim Wing was angry. *We got it all dirty.*

The Lightning Papers, Jim Wing

AIR

The Cosmological Power of Attraction pervades all things in the universe. We remain on the surface of the Earth because of the gravitational attraction between Earth and our bodies. Further, we are living inside an electromagnetic field. Even beyond that, each of us *is* an electromagnetic field. We move through the cosmos as a unit of centrated mass which is capable of experiencing extreme attraction anytime, anywhere, in any given split second.

Visonary Cosmology

AIR

L ove can happen instantly. In a lightning flash love can become the thing we live and die for, the organizing principle of our lives.

Visionary Cosmology

AIR

May inner hearing open to reveal the vibration of the sacred Word, the Word by which all is created, sustained, destroyed, the sacred vibration at the heart of moved and unmoved alike. May the voice of the sacred be in me and with me, and may that sacred voice sing out as the vibratory power of Love. May I know that Love is the Word. Love binds, maintains, and destroys to heal.

Kabbalah and Tarot of the Spirit, The Tower

AIR

P hantoms from the past appear. What have they come to teach? Danger, Cruelty, Desolation, Despair, Pain, then Learning and Breaking the Chains of Dysfunctional Patterning. It is time to open your eyes to all that has happened. There is the trigger… and we remember. Our challenge is to not look away. Our challenge is to "turn on the screen" and call back the horrible instant. Through active engagement, we can transcend entrapments that have held us in a state of victimization; stunted identity. Ask the monster, What do I need to learn?

Kabbalah and Tarot of the Spirit, 9 of Wind

AIR

T his is the powerful sphere of healing. When we work actively to heal the wounds of past and present, we become newly embraced in the open heart of cosmological Love. We realize once again that Love is the only enduring form of protection. Love is the only power that is completely unassailable. Love is the surging power that conquers the monstrous head of fear.

Kabbalah and Tarot of the Spirit, 9 of Wind

AIR

W e are designed to receive and radiate light and sound. In fact, any being who looks upon us with pupils that receive photons receives our energy – wittingly or unwittingly.

Visionary Cosmology

AIR

H ow many social philosophers exist in the human community? *Seven billion.* As universe itself in the power of its own creation, each of us has the ability to reflect upon our philosophies and actions. As individuals and as groups we can decide, within existing conditions, how we will take action.

The Lightning Papers

AIR

Do you realize that we are a species that has only just now awakened to the extent of our own destruction as a homicidal and suicidal force upon this planet? Do you realize that we have only just now realized the extent of the ecocide we have committed? We have only just realized we are actually destroying our own habitat, or, rather, the very loam that gave rise to us and to which we shall return. But I have hope. Sociological studies show that, in the situation of a crisis, if no one moves, everyone will stay still, but if one person makes even the slightest gesture toward helping, suddenly everyone floods in to help.

The Lightning Papers, Anastasia West

AIR

E very single moment and every single relationship hold the magic of transcendental possibilities.

The Lightning Papers

AIR

Negative past influences may be affecting the present without due cause. It is time to clear out, see clearly, begin with new energy. The standard of action must emerge from within yourself.

Tarot of the Spirit, The Chariot

AIR

W isdom, I can nearly hear your call – a whisper – through the veil. You speak in tongues awakening fields of consciousness: the preserving, protecting power of words, new words as yet unsaid, words that manifest and edge through the bony fence encasing matters of the heart; words that dart through pillars from the middle of the soul. The strength of will is measured by the will to let the Force of Life manifest unreined. The strength of will is hearing through the water well enough to speak the Secret of the Flame.

Tarot of the Spirit, The Chariot

AIR

T he strength of your volition is surrender. You must understand that you *are* moving in the flow of the cosmic will and you must let the cosmic spirit find unobstructed manifestation through you. This means you must trust your deepest intuition. As your gift is revealed, you will see that you have created it. In right communion you *are* the creative force.

Tarot of the Spirit, The Chariot

AIR

May I remember I contain the Great Mystery. May I remember that the matrix of all that has been, is, and ever shall be, is in me and with me. May I remember that the pattern of all Creation is within, is here, is Now. May I occupy the Inner Temple, following the guiding Star into freedom, into love, into truth, and with the fullest cosmic accord.

Kabbalah and Tarot of the Spirit, The Star

AIR

C ome all the treasure
    Velvet, diamonds
Of Night's windsome sky
Springs a message from Her depths
Springs a lovenote from Her thighs:
    Thy Star doth riseth, Dear One,
    Dances Magic in Thine Eyes!

Tarot of the Spirit, The Star

AIR

W e are made of the essence of our planet, Earth, which was birthed by our star, our Sun, which stands in relationship to all the other stars in our galaxy. We are one with that which made us. We contain the starseed structure of past, future, and Now. Now is the time to remember who you really are. Now is the time to claim your space as the star essence of the Cosmos.

Kabbalah and Tarot of the Spirit, The Star

AIR

Give up to gain. Surrender in order to achieve. Recognize that all that is good has the potential for evil; all that is evil has the potential for good. You are the great decider.

Tarot of the Spirit, 3 of Wind

AIR

T o shift perspectives requires gaining new knowledge whereby we can begin to restructure our foundations so as to actively create a new worldview. We realize through this process that the human universe is not "just the way it is." Things are *not* as they seem. As we awaken to the realization that we are universe living the path of its own self-discovery, we begin to realize the profound context and nature in which all aspects of existence are interwoven.

Visionary Cosmology

AIR

All emerges from the ever-living Fire of Oneness which takes innumerable shapes and names. The Fiery One changes and yet remains immutable. It never increases or diminishes or loses its eternal nature. Of its permutations there is no end. Therefore, everything is new. Everything is now. See? Wild river of flame that you are, you will never step into the same river twice.

The Lightning Papers, Anastasia West on Heraclitus

AIR

T hrough withdrawing, all things become clear. Take a break and remember, "still waters run deep."

Tarot of the Spirit, 8 of Water

AIR

Y ou, alone, are the master craftsman of your life. With the power of love, you become the master craftsman of the universe.

Tarot of the Spirit, 8 of Water

AIR

W ith the power of keen thought, Wind Sister has the capacity to change the world. Seeking the depths of truth through intense and honest introspection, Wind Sister enters into the domain of highest conscience. She becomes the power of Idea, the manifestation of the indwelling divine, in the process of materialization. Thus, Wind Sister is the Radiant Sister activating the power of conscious self-reflection to find meaning and to participate in developing the course of the Cosmos.

Kabbalah and Tarot of the Spirit, Wind Sister

AIR

She is original and she originates. As such, she wields awesome power. Her sword – her intellect – is fine, sharp, clean and clear. It goes directly to the point. With her sword she rends the veil that obscures and entraps, thus setting the immortal soul free. She comes wielding her sword to rend the veils for Love. Love is her passion which, in the end, conquers all.

Kabbalah and Tarot of the Spirit, Wind Sister

AIR

W omen *are* the infinite realm of darkness, the infinite fabric of being, the matrix, the implicate order, the monad and the holomovement. We are the birth-givers of the cosmos, the universe giving birth to ourselves and also to men. The woman bears the body of the future. That's why women are always working for peace.

The Lightning Papers, Trishetta Parker

AIR

Do they teach you about babies? Do they teach you about dying? Do they teach you how to love? No? If they don't teach you these things, what could you possibly be learning?

The Lightning Papers, Janet Herrera's mother

AIR

Adaptation is the emergence of a trait that helps an individual or a species survive in a particular set of conditions, a particular environment or habitat. Adaptation refers to physiological mutations in structure, function or form such as the adaptation of horse teeth to grinding grass. It can also refer to changes in behavior which are not genetic in nature as when a cat, who doesn't like water, learns to swim to catch fish.

The question is: What wants to happen?

Visionary Cosmology

AIR

Before we humans could have eyes to see, the eye had to be created. That took millions of years. Before we humans could have ears to hear, the ear had to be created. That took millions of years also. Eventually, there emerged a creature who could paint pictures, make fire, imagine how to hunt, how to farm, how to work metal, how to use money, and how to symbolize the world in the form of writing and mathematics.

The question is: What will we see? What will we hear? What will we make of it all?

The Lightning Papers, Anastasia West

AIR

A s people wake up to the fact that the universe is not 'out there' somewhere, and that human society, just like the universe, does not exist 'out there' somewhere, but, that, as humans, we make up our world everyday of our lives through the choices we make, we will become empowered to create whole new ways of imagining the future.

The question is: What is really important to you?

The Lightning Papers, Anastasia West

AIR

Sequence. Causation. Order out of chaos. Chaos out of order. The human impulse to understand the nature of being. The desperate desire to grasp the mystery. To control the unknown forces, pin down the wild butterflies, describe, categorize, rank. To tame the future. That's all about fear, isn't it?

Does the universe love us? Do we love ourselves?

The Lightning Papers, Anastasia West

AIR

C ultivated fields will eventually bloom. Love every stick, stone, plant and animal and you will experience great bounty. Be diligent in attuning to every detail of the work required as you tend your "garden." Rejoice in your life and help to create a joyous life for others.

Tarot of the Spirit, Earth Mother

AIR

May my inner eye be open to the vision that heals. May I see with the light of spirit. May I see with the heart of compassion. May I realize that all error moves me closer to the Target of Perfection. May I integrate that knowledge. May I live my life with the clarity that Cosmic Vision will unfold: the knowledge that all things – including the difficult – are part of the great whole.

Kabbalah and Tarot of the Spirit, The Devil

AIR

Stay on your path. Everything is coming to fruition. A miraculous birth is at hand. To resist this great birth would bring pain. Giving birth to the "children" of body or mind is not easy, but it will be rewarding. Let your "child" be a product of love.

Tarot of the Spirit, 3 of Fire

AIR

T he Universe.
One verse, one turn, one Song
Hailed on Earth as it is in Heaven
One Will
Done on Earth as it is in Heaven
One Life
Lived on Earth as it is in Heaven.

Tarot of the Spirit, The Universe

AIR

R ediscoverig the reason for incarnation is the message. You are the growing Love of the Cosmos; you are growing the Love of the Universe.

Kabbalah and Tarot of the Spirit, 6 of Water

AIR

Y ou are worried. You feel physically deprived. You feel poor. Your soul is hungry. You are tense. Your body is stressed. Your equilibrium is off. You feel unbalanced. You feel defeated. It is as if you have been left out in the cold. Unwittingly, you have created a reality that has denied your inner self. You may not yet realize it, but a new light has been ignited on the level of spirit. It will light your way. You have the opportunity, right now, to examine the active volcano of Self from the edge of the crater. See truth. See it bravely.

Tarot of the Spirit, 5 of Earth

AIR

Fear inhabits the unknown. Fear, Tension, Pain, Anxiety, Inhibition, Immobilization, Weakness, Depletion, then Surrender, Imagination and Advancement with Awe. Realize that fear is your adversary and also your friend and motivator. You are being called to realign your efforts; to redirect the power of your imagination. This is not the time to allow fear to disempower you. Replace fear with awe. Move forward in faith. A world of possibility awaits you. The Key to Transcendence is at Hand.

Kabbalah and Tarot of the Spirit, 5 of Wind

AIR

W hat if who I am is not the form, this form, this body, this changing shape, this identity I appear to be? What if I have always been alive since the beginning? What if I am universe itself in the process of its own creation? Who am I? Who have I been? What will I become? What if I am immortal?

The Lightning Papers, Anastasia West

AIR

W*hat is a soul anyway? And what do particles and waves in the universe have to do with a man's soul?* Henri was waiting for some kind of revelation that made sense. He was trying to remember what his father, the pastor, had said, but only one thing kept surfacing, *My soul, wait in silence for God only, for my hope is from Him. He only is my rock and my salvation, my stronghold, and I shall not be shaken.*

The Lightning Papers, Henri du Par

AIR

Y ou are in a holding pattern. Having now mastered a difficult task, you are resting on your laurels. Only you know that disturbing influences are beginning to emerge. There is a tendency to cling to successes because of ego. Be careful: clinging to the desires of ego can be a deadly enemy. The things that gratify the ego do not necessarily gratify the soul.

Tarot of the Spirit, 4 of Wind

AIR

I hold my future in my own curved hand. May I access Cosmic Light. May I access Cosmic Love. May I veil to seek Cosmic Vision. May I heal and become whole. May I heed the spiritual call and embark upon the path that leads to the center of the temple, the temple built on the deepest well: spring of Light, of Love, of Understanding.

Kabbalah and Tarot of the Spirit, The Wheel of Fortune

AIR

F ortune was a goddess. It was said she could bring about alternations or reversals in the world of human affairs. She turned the Wheel of Fortune as she saw fit – sometimes mischievously. The Wheel encompassed poverty and riches, war and peace, passion and patience, glory and humility – each pair residing across from one another. The Wheel was in continual spin. You could be rich one day – and poor the next. But, when we occupy the Wheel as a spiritual seeker, we step off the rim. We move toward the center, which is the heart of the Universe, and also the heart of our Self. The closer we get to center, the slower the Wheel seems to turn. We know we have finally arrived the moment we encounter the subtly vibrating stillness of balance.

Kabbalah and Tarot of the Spirit, The Wheel of Fortune

AIR

I n opening to the more expansive Real, we begin to receive and contain all the mystical beneficence of the Cosmos – which is all around us, and which we *are*. Here, then, is eternal Victory. True victory lies in realizing center, the place where all apparent opposites are integrated into One. Here is the heart of the Cosmos, the realization of blessed being, the true and absolute wealth of *being* Universal Soul.

Kabbalah and Tarot of the Spirit, The Wheel of Fortune

AIR

THE COSMIC QUARTET

The quotes in *Days of Spirit* come from the Cosmic Quartet by Pamela Eakins. These four books are dedicated to cosmological realization. They include: *Tarot of the Spirit, Kabbalah and Tarot of the Spirit, The Lightning Papers: Ten Powers of Evolution* and *Visionary Cosmology: The New Paradigm*.

ABOUT THE AUTHOR

Dr. Pamela Eakins is a Sociologist and Visionary Cosmologist. She has taught at Stanford University, the University of Colorado and the California Institute of Integral Studies. She is the founder and director of Pacific Center. Her books include:

Tarot of the Spirit
Kabbalah and Tarot of the Spirit
The Lightning Papers, 10 Powers of Evolution
Visionary Cosmology, The New Paradigm
Mothers in Transition
The American Way of Birth
Passages for a Spiritual Birth
Priestess
Heart, Breath and Graceful Movement
Love Sonnets
Cosmic Interiors

Classes, Consultation, Events: www.pamelaeakins.net

Made in United States
Orlando, FL
03 March 2022